INTERNAL
GRADUA

"Are you a Christian?" Such a simple question!
What does it really mean?
Here is your opportunity to find the answer,
based on the authority of Scripture.
You will learn about basic doctrines of Christianity
and how they relate to living today.
You will find a depth of interpretation that will give
you a new awareness of God at work in your life.
You will see what God has done
and continues to do for you to bring about
your complete salvation.

What's God been doing

all this time?

by David Allan Hubbard

A Division of G/L Publications
Glendale, California, U.S.A.

Scripture quotations from the RSV of the Bible, Copyrighted 1946 and 1952, Division of Christian Education, NCCC, U.S.A. Used by permission.

© Copyright 1970 by G/L Publications
Printed in U.S.A.
All rights reserved.

Published by
Regal Books Division, G/L Publications
Glendale, California 91209, U.S.A.

Library of Congress Catalog Card No. 70-122885
ISBN 0-8307-0083-8

INTERNATIONAL CHRISTIAN
GRADUATE UNIVERSITY

BX
6333
H875w
1970

Contents

A teaching and discussion guide for use with this book
is available from your church supplier.

17014

A special word of thanks is due my nephew, the Reverend Robert L. Hubbard, Jr., who has gently and skillfully shepherded this manuscript from the oral form of the radio talks to its present state. Without his help publication would have been impossible.

In many and various ways God spoke of old to our fathers by the prophets; but in these last days he has spoken to us by a Son, whom he appointed the heir of all things, through whom also he created the world. He reflects the glory of God and bears the very stamp of his nature, upholding the universe by his word of power. When he made purification for sins, he sat down at the right hand of the Majesty on high.
Hebrews 1:1—3

CHAPTER 1
What the Bible Is All About

"What's the Bible all about?" Has anyone ever asked you that question? If so, how did you answer? A book of spiritual principles? A collection of ethical and moral instructions? A guide to life? Maybe you can make a case for these descriptions of the Bible, but they tend to be a bit wide of the target.

What is the Bible all about? It is about *God*. It is not an abstract essay or treatise, nor a collection of theological theories, but a story, the history of what God is doing.

3

And what is God doing? He is saving a people to serve him. He is in the rescue business, and he has been throughout history. Before the first man and woman shuffled out of the Garden, chagrined at the thought of their sin, God sought them in their hiding and clothed their naked shame.

From that point on, step by step, he executed his grand deliverance. Noah and his family were snatched from the watery grave of judgment. Abraham was given a solemn pledge, a covenant, of a land that he would possess, a nation that he would father, and a blessing that he would convey to all the families of the earth.

These promises were reaffirmed, moreover, to the next two generations, Isaac and Jacob. Even a long and arduous season of captivity in Egypt did not derail God's saving program. After the centuries of bondage came the day of deliverance. And God saw to it that Moses was on hand to lead the sons of Abraham, Isaac and Jacob out of slavery.

The Great Rescuer was at work. Plagues harassed the Egyptian pharaoh, whom his subjects considered to be divine. His weak humanity was laid bare by the power of Israel's God. His army was routed by the swirling waters of a sea that moments before had parted to let God's people pass.

The Great Rescuer continued to work. The mighty desert enemies, hunger and thirst, were defeated by the power of God during four long decades of wilderness wandering. Joshua succeeded Moses as leader. Hostile tribes were put to flight, and the people were settled in their new land. Two-thirds of Abraham's promise had been

4

fulfilled: God had formed a nation of Abraham's family, and he had granted them a homeland of their own.

The third part of the promise, however, took a while longer to complete, but the saving God was at work all the while. He set up a kingdom in the new land under David and Solomon. Even when the people disobeyed him, his saving power was present. Salvation was his business, though sometimes he had strange ways of conducting it.

Once he sent his people into exile and put in jeopardy the very promises he had made to Abraham. He removed them from their land and threatened their national existence. He destroyed the capital city he had captured for them and the temple where he had committed himself to dwell.

But again his work of rescue went on, and he brought them back to resettle their land and to rebuild their nation. But failure and disobedience were still their way of life. They treated his law lightly and took his love for granted.

A more drastic solution was required if God was to have a people who would live to praise and serve him. What the people of Israel and the whole human family needed was a fresh start—a new lease on life. A new beginning of relationship with God had to be made.

So God sent his Son and named him Jesus, the Savior, the new Joshua (Jesus and Joshua are the same name) who would lead his people into a new land of rest and security. Jesus is called "Savior," and save he does. What the great leaders of the past were not able to do, Jesus has done. He has raised up a people who love and serve God. He has given them a fresh start, and his power will see them through to complete salvation, to full fellowship with God. In him the third part of Abraham's promise is fulfilled: All nations can find strength and blessing through him.[1]

The New Testament is the official account of what God has done for the human family through Jesus, and it also gives us specific aspects of his work—"bright facets of salvation" we sometimes call them. They amplify in detail the meaning of what God has been doing in history. Together they form a metaphorical prism which refracts the light of God's movement in history into a glittering rainbow of explanation—the explanation of who God is and what it means to know him. That's what the Bible is all about. And that's what this book is all about.

These "bright facets" are important not only because they explain what God has done for man through Jesus, but also because they show us how we are to talk about God. We can't go around making up our own metaphors or images of God. To do so might put us in danger of breaking the commandment against idolatry. Distorted and perverted verbal images of God are just as idolatrous as graven images. Metaphors unworthy of God's majesty and unrepresentative of his greatness are just as much an affront to God as images of wood and stone. They may encourage a further affront—distorted worship.

So how can we talk about God in earthly language? The answer is this: we listen to the ways in which God speaks about himself in the Bible. Father, Shepherd, King, Judge, Husband, Potter, Farmer—these and other expressions, when rightly understood and considered together, give us the facets of God's personality. Not that we can know all about God, but we can know enough to trust and love him. Our knowledge may not be complete, but we are assured that his Word is accurate and will not lead us astray.

The same situation applies when it comes to speaking of God's great acts of salvation—the ways he bridged the gap between himself and man. There is no celestial language to describe the new things God has done. We are hedged in with human words. But God in the Scriptures has chosen some apt word pictures, some graphic figures of speech, some marvelous metaphors to describe what he has done.

And that's what this book is all about. It explores the metaphors God uses to explain the meaning of his deeds in human history. They are the "bright facets of salvation," and they are what the Bible is all about. At the conclusion of each chapter is a prayer response to that chapter's theme. You may want to make these prayers personal by rephrasing them in your own words and offering them as your own prayer to God. It's hoped that they will encourage you to experience God's work of salvation in your own life. That, too, is what the Bible is all about.

Prayer: Heavenly Father, you began your great rescue operation long ago, and you have been faith-

7

fully carrying it out ever since. You've spelled out the meaning of your program in detail through the Bible. Brighten my hopelessly darkened mind with rays of understanding refracted by your "bright facets of salvation"—the full-blown explanation of all the exciting, thrilling things you've done for your people. And lead me to participate in your program, to experience your salvation. Through Jesus Christ, the great Savior. Amen.

Now there was a man of the Pharisees, named Nicodemus, a ruler of the Jews. This man came to Jesus by night and said to him, "Rabbi, we know that you are a teacher come from God; for no one can do these signs that you do, unless God is with him." Jesus answered him, "Truly, truly, I say to you, unless one is born anew, he cannot see the kingdom of God." Nicodemus said to him, "How can a man be born when he is old? Can he enter a second time into his mother's womb and be born?" Jesus answered, "Truly, truly, I say to you, unless one is born of water and the Spirit, he cannot enter the kingdom of God. That which is born of the flesh is flesh, and that which is born of the Spirit is spirit. Do not marvel that I said to you, 'You must be born anew.' The wind blows where it wills, and you hear the sound of it, but you do not know whence it comes or whither it goes; so it is with every one who is born of the Spirit." Nicodemus said to him, "How can this be?" Jesus answered him, "Are you a teacher of Israel, and yet you do not understand this? Truly, truly, I say to you, we speak of what we know, and bear witness to what we have seen; but you do not receive our testimony. If I have told you earthly things and you do not believe, how can you believe if I tell you heavenly things? No one has ascended into heaven but he who descended from heaven, the Son of man. And as Moses lifted up the serpent in the wilderness, so must the Son of man be lifted up, that whoever believes in him may have eternal life."
John 3:1—15

CHAPTER 2
A Fresh Start: The New Birth

Most of us live in grooves that are rapidly becoming ruts. How long since you made a really drastic change in your pattern of life? We are creatures of habit. We get up at the same time each day and go through long-established routines until we ready ourselves for bed and a night's rest which prepares us to endure the same routines the next day.

Once in a while we try to break out of the mold, but usually without much success. We are confined in the clutches of habit. But worse yet, we are held in the grips of sin. We try to do better but cannot.

11

We resolve to change, but then settle back again into our old comfortable ways.

Every human being since Adam has needed a fresh start. The problem is universal. It's good for us to remember this because we tend to think that only the obvious failures in life require a fresh start. A drunk sits hunched on the steps of a tenement building. A teen-aged girl writhes in uncontrollable convulsions from drug withdrawal. A criminal quietly watches the world's activities through windows framed with stone and steel. And we say, "If only *they* could begin again!"

Here is where Jesus exposes our blind spots. His conversation with Nicodemus comments directly on this problem.

Human Birth Is No Substitute for Spiritual Birth

Jesus wasted no time getting to the heart of the matter. His first statement to the devout and learned Jewish teacher was direct and plain: "You and everyone like you has to be born all over again if you are to come to terms with God."[1]

It was not Nicodemus' intellectual brilliance that made him see that no man could return to the womb for this fresh start; it was his common sense. We all know that it's physically impossible to be reborn. Jesus went on to make clear that he wasn't talking about a new physical birth. In fact, he makes the point forcefully that *human birth is no substitute for spiritual birth*. Like begets like. Sinful human beings beget sinful beings. A new kind of birth is called for.

12

Human birth does not equip us with all we need to serve God. There's a built-in defect of selfishness that we cannot overcome on our own. There's no steady transition, no evolutionary process that takes our earthly life and spiritualizes it. Jesus said, "That which is born of the flesh is flesh, and that which is born of the Spirit is spirit."[2] Flesh cannot become spirit by some kind of religious alchemy.

And there is no human way of starting over and making real headway in knowing God. Nicodemus was right. Humanly speaking, a second birth is a monstrous impossibility.

According to Jesus, however, another kind of second birth is possible. Jesus calls it being "born of water and the Spirit."[3] Water here probably symbolizes repentance as it did in the baptism practiced by John the Baptist. Repentance is renouncing our old way of doing things: rejecting God and trusting in ourselves. And opening ourselves to God's new way, the way of his Spirit—God's power and presence working in us. This radical change, this drastic alteration of our basic attitude toward life, is so sweeping that Jesus dramatically labels it "a new birth."

Knowledge Is No Substitute for Experience

Nicodemus was a rabbi, perhaps one of the top officials in Judaism. He was perceptive enough to see that God's power was radiating through Jesus. He was open enough to seek conversation with Jesus. Yet his vast and accurate knowledge was not enough to give him the second birth.

13

For him entering the Kingdom of God (that is, coming to know God's power and glory) was a matter of doing right things. For Jesus, however, it was a matter of committing oneself to the right person: the one whose sole purpose was to give us life.

Knowledge is helpful. But knowledge without full trust in Jesus Christ will lead us away from God's Kingdom—not toward it.

Two Words of Warning Are in Order

First, Jesus is not talking about just any spiritual experience. He's not talking about a mystical encounter or ecstatic thrill. He's not talking about a trip stimulated by meditation or drugs. Rather, Jesus is describing a specifically Christian reality. He's talking about an experience produced by God's coming to live in a person's life.

This experience is based on the authority of Jesus' word. Only he, the Son of man descended from heaven,[4] knows the whole plan of God. His credentials are impeccable. When it comes to knowing God, we listen to him and to no one else. And this fresh start for the human family is made possible only because Christ was lifted up to die on the cross.

Jesus told Nicodemus that "as Moses lifted up the serpent in the wilderness, so must the Son of man be lifted up, that whoever believes in him may have eternal life."[5]

Nicodemus knew the familiar Old Testament story to which Jesus referred. The children of

Israel had become impatient with the way God was handling their escape from Egypt. They blamed God for their lack of food and water. God became angry and sent fiery serpents from whose poisonous bite many people died.

But the people repented and begged for forgiveness. God instructed Moses to make a serpent of bronze and to set it on a pole. He promised that if anyone who had suffered a serpent's bite would look at the raised bronze serpent, he would immediately be healed. Many looked and were healed.[6]

Jesus used this story to paint a beautiful picture of his own work on behalf of the human family. He was lifted up on a cross "that whoever believes in him may have eternal life." In the cross of Christ, and nowhere else, is there healing for us all. He was crucified to pay the penalty for our sin so that if we look to him, accepting what he has done for us, we will be healed of the mortal wound of sin which paralyzes our ability to please God. We receive a fresh start in life—a new birth.

The second word of warning is that we should not wait to understand all that Jesus meant before we commit ourselves to him. For years a friend of mine had attended church with his wife but had made no commitment to Christ. He was a spectator but not a participant in things Christian. One day in Sunday School class I said, "If you wait for all your problems to be solved before you accept Jesus as Lord, you'll never make it. Come to him and let him solve the problems." That week my friend's life was turned around; he made his fresh start by trusting Christ. You can do the same.

15

Now is the time for you to make a fresh start, for God to begin his brand new, his bright new, beautiful work in your life. Talk to him about it. Tell him you want a new start in life; you want to know him.

Prayer: Father, you made everything new at the beginning when you created the world and all of us in it. Make me new again as I call upon you. Bring to my broken, stained, disfigured life the freshness of your new creation. Through your Son, Jesus Christ. Amen.

Jesus said to them, "Truly, truly, I say to you, the Son can do nothing of his own accord, but only what he sees the Father doing; for whatever he does, that the Son does likewise. For the Father loves the Son, and shows him all that he himself is doing; and greater works than these will he show him, that you may marvel. For as the Father raises the dead and gives them life, so also the Son gives life to whom he will. The Father judges no one, but has given all judgment to the Son, that all may honor the Son, even as they honor the Father. He who does not honor the Son does not honor the Father who sent him. Truly, truly, I say to you, he who hears my word and believes him who sent me, has eternal life; he does not come into judgment, but has passed from death to life.

"Truly, truly, I say to you, the hour is coming, and now is, when the dead will hear the voice of the Son of God, and those who hear will live. For as the Father has life in himself, so he has granted the Son also to have life in himself, and has given him authority to execute judgment, because he is the Son of man. Do not marvel at this; for the hour is coming when all who are in the tombs will hear his voice and come forth, those who have done good, to the resurrection of life, and those who have done evil, to the resurrection of judgment."
John 5:19—29

CHAPTER 3

Linked to the Age to Come:
Eternal Life

"Ah, this is the life!" When have you heard or said these words? Standing at the edge of a sparkling stream, casting with a fly rod to hook a glistening trout? Basking in the Mediterranean sun on the deck of a white liner threading its way among the Greek islands? Or just sitting relaxed in your living room watching the children play Monopoly?

What is your definition of living? Is it hiking in the Rockies while the setting sun paints the clouds and snowcapped peaks its changing shades of crimson? Is it strolling through fields of wheat and gently feeling the heads of golden grain? Is it a drive through the pine forest with a loved one by your side?

What catches the essence of life for you? For some it is in the excitement of driving too fast playing too hard, drinking too much. For others it is the homey comfort of a family circle, warming itself by an autumn fire. For still others it is the thrill of achievement: a project completed, a business built up, a scoring record broken, a pie beautifully baked.

The trouble with these expressions of life is that they are too limited, too restricting. They tie the heart of life to things that are temporary. We cannot fish or sail all the time. Our families grow up and move away. We may not have the money to travel to exotic places or the energy to tackle difficult projects and see them through to success.

Yet all of us want to live, and we want to live now. Intuitively we sense the emptiness, the hollowness of much of our living. Desperately we seek to brighten the dull routines which hold us in their grips. Our motive may be right, but our response is usually wrong. We want to live, live to the full. And live we should. But we are trapped by wrong definitions. Our understanding of what life really is is so limited that our lives are steered in the wrong direction. Our maps are inadequate, and the road signs are incorrect at worst and hard to read at best.

The result is that we are lost. That's a harsh word, one that would send shudders of terror down our spines were we to hear it in the woods or on the desert.

But lost we are, trying to kindle sparks of meaning in the wet wood of which our lives are made. We take the soggy stick of our work or business and try to rub it against the soaked twig of our leisure to generate some spark with which to light a flickering fire of authenticity in our lives. We rub till our hands are blistered, our arms are weary, and we scarcely stir a puff of smoke.

We have lost meaning in our work and find only fleeting pleasure in our leisure. No wonder our life lacks even sparks of meaning.

It's to set our lives ablaze with purpose that God sent Jesus Christ. Look how plainly Jesus put it: "I came that they might have life, and have it abundantly."[1] On our own we barely eke out an existence. Jesus gives abundant life.

Eternal Life Begins with New Birth

In the preceding chapter we saw how this all begins. A fresh start through a new birth is our Lord's answer. The conversation with the learned Jewish teacher, Nicodemus, warns us that no one, no matter how lofty his station or how able his person, can come to terms with God without this start. And Jesus' conversation with the woman at the well in Samaria[2] encourages us that no one, no matter how lowly his position or degraded his circumstance, is beyond starting. God loves the world, and that includes all of us.

A fresh start is possible because God has sent Jesus to heal our past, to change our aims, and to set our thinking straight. And this fresh start, this wonderfully drastic change which is called "a new birth," leads to a new brand of life—"abundant life" or "eternal life" is the way the Bible describes it.

The important thing about this life, however, is not its length. Of course, it lasts forever, and we rejoice in the thought. But if our new life were not radically different from the old one, would we really want to live forever?

Eternal Life Brings a New Quality of Life

Both abundant life and eternal life speak of *quality* more than *quantity*. The literal meaning of eternal life is "the life of the age to come." This deserves clarification.

In Jesus' day it was customary to divide reality into two great categories—this age and the age to come. This age is our present worldly existence with its trials and temptations, its possibilities and pitfalls; it is life as we now know it, checkered, marred, mixed.

The age to come, on the other hand, is the future age when God's glory will be known by all men and all of God's purposes will be achieved. It's the time when the imperfections and injustices of the present age are reversed and sin and death are done away with.

Jesus clearly recognized these two categories—this age and the age to come. The Master gives his disciples promise of reward for their sacrifices in these words: "There is no one who has left house or brothers or sisters or mother or father or children or lands, for my sake and for the gospel, who will not receive a hundredfold now in this time, houses and brothers and sisters and mothers and children and lands, with persecutions, and in the age to come eternal life."³ Rewards come "now in this time" and "in the age to come," the two great spheres of reality.

The important point made in our text from John's Gospel is that we can know the life of the age to come right now in this life, in this age. Eternal life is not just a future hope; it is a present reality.

And it is a present reality because Christ has come. The Son who shares the Father's life has brought that life to men. The age to come is present in the here and now. The glory of heaven is seen on earth. The person of God himself is revealed among men. The wonder of eternity is made known in the midst of our times. Abundant life is available in a context of sin and death.

Eternal Life Brings a New Experience

Let's dig deeper into the meaning of eternal life, the life of the age to come. It is, first of all, an *experience of restoration*. The age to come is the time when God's will is "done on earth as it is in heaven," a time when his kingdom comes in all its fullness, a time when all the damage done by sin and death is reversed.

The clearest expression of this is the final resurrection of the dead. Death, which has reigned so long as king of human life and destiny, is defeated. Death, which reminds us constantly of the sin with which its reign began and the sins which have aided its cause since the beginning, is itself put to death because God raises the dead. The damage and dissolution, the decay and corruption, which are death's constant companions, are disinherited. They thought they held the key to human destiny, but they were wrong. God raises the dead.

The astounding claim of the gospel is that this resurrection power by which God will rob every grave of its apparent victory is present in the midst of men through Jesus Christ: "For as the Father raises the dead and gives them life, so also the Son gives life to whom he will."⁴ And again: "For as the Father has life in himself, so he has granted the Son also to have life in himself."⁵ This life-giving power which caused the earth to bring forth living things, which has kept them going ever since, and which will frame a new heaven and a new earth at the end, is at work in Jesus of Nazareth. And part of what is meant by eternal life is access to this power.

A second aspect of eternal life is *relief from judgment*. The age to come is a time when God's judgment will be complete and all of life's injustices, inequities, and inconsistencies will be dealt with. Men of faith in Jesus' day knew that God stood ready to judge, and they dreaded that judgment day.

What they did not know until Jesus came along, however, was that Jesus himself is the judge. "The Father judges no one, but has given all judgment to the Son, that all may honor the Son, even as they honor the Father."⁶

And he who has authority to judge also has authority to release from judgment those who meet God's terms. How he does this is not discussed in this passage, but other New Testament passages tell us that Jesus himself bears our judgment when he dies on the cross.[7] We shall see how in the next chapter. But here the crucial point is that Christ, the judge, exempts from judgment those who trust him: "Truly, truly, I say to you, he who hears my word and believes in him who sent me, has eternal life; he does not come into judgment, but has passed from death to life."[8]

Think of the release, the freedom, that Jesus is offering! The fear of death and judgment is erased! Eternal life becomes our present possession! We enter into the beauty and glory of the age to come right here and now!

One other aspect of eternal life shines through our text. This abundant life is *participation in divine love*. The Father not only honors the Son by turning the gavel of judgment over to him, and he not only shares the power to create life with the Son, but he fellowships with him in perpetual love and opens his deepest secrets to him: "For the Father loves the Son, and shows him all that he . . . is doing."[9] When the Father and Son share their life and power with the believer, they also share their love. To know that you are loved by God, that your life is wrapped in a bundle of fellowship with Christ and other believers, is part of eternal life. It's a life of love from which nothing—not even death—can separate us.[10]

And better yet, all of this is given to us by Jesus who "gives life to whom he will."[11] We could not buy it, borrow it, earn it, or steal it. It is God's gift. Power, freedom and love belong to him alone. These are the stuff of eternal life.

Our joy and privilege are to hear and believe; that is, to treat with full seriousness and to trust with full commitment. God's offer is current. God's power is sufficient. God's grace is magnificent. This is the life! Accept no substitutes!

Prayer: Our Father, I am amazed at the nature, the beauty, and the duration of eternal life. All around I see doubt, doom, and death. Grant me this gracious gift, that I may make that grand transfer from death to life. Through Jesus Christ. Amen.

But now the righteousness of God has been manifested apart from law, although the law and the prophets bear witness to it, the righteousness of God through faith in Jesus Christ for all who believe. For there is no distinction; since all have sinned and fall short of the glory of God, they are justified by his grace as a gift, through the redemption which is in Christ Jesus, whom God put forward as an expiation by his blood, to be received by faith. This was to show God's righteousness, because in his divine forbearance he had passed over former sins; it was to prove at the present time that he himself is righteous and that he justifies him who has faith in Jesus.

Romans 3:21—26

CHAPTER 4

Cleared in Court:
Justification

The courtroom is jammed to capacity. Muffled murmurs of conversation await the sentence about to be pronounced. In front, the convicted assailant blindly stares at the floor oblivious of the swirl of speculation which surrounds him. The scales of justice did not balance in his favor. His future now rests in the hands of the judge.

Conversations cease as the judge enters. The piercing silence of anticipation is unbearable. The judge nervously adjusts his glasses, clears his throat, and addresses the guilty man.

"You have been found guilty as charged, and this court will now carry out its duty by imposing a sentence commensurate with the crime."

Utter silence.

"For crimes against this society, this court sentences you to die in the state penitentiary."

Light conversation voices society's satisfaction

with the sentence. The condemned man shows no visible response.

"However," the judge continues, "this court mercifully orders that the defendant be acquitted of this charge and his record cleared of all other convictions. He is now a free man."

"Unfair," you say? Yes, by our standards of justice it is unfair. If a judge did that today we might call him crooked and think the trial was rigged. Yet God in his love and grace has done just that. When God saves us, he clears us in court. He acquits us even though we deserved judgment. And this act is central to our relationship with God. *Justification* we call it.

The Verdict—God's Pronouncement of Guilt

There is no doubt about our guilt. The Bible makes clear just how culpable we are before God. The first three chapters of Paul's letter to the Romans, for instance, tell us unequivocally that all of us have sinned and come short of God's glory. And when we come to Romans 3:19, we read that every mouth is stopped from offering excuses and the whole world is held accountable to God. The verdict on the human family is "Guilty!"—and in court when the verdict is "guilty," the sentence usually follows. Not so with God.

The Cross—God's Announcement of Love

Romans 3:21 goes on to tell us that the righteousness of God is revealed in the midst of our guilt.

The following verses declare that God has worked out a way to justify those who should be condemned. The death of Jesus on the cross is the basis of our justification. Paul made this clear. Christ pays the penalty. We are cleared, we are declared righteous, we are counted as guiltless before God because our sins have been judged in Jesus Christ. We never have to face our sin and our failure again.

The text goes on to tell us that God accepts the penalty Christ has paid and yet remains just. God could not overlook sin. He could not simply say, "Oh, forget about it and go your own way. I didn't really mean it when I said that is wrong." God is not bluffing when he talks about judgment. History is moving toward judgment, toward a day of final reckoning. Disaster and punishment may come along the way to remind us of the ultimate judgment we face. But the point of the cross is this: in Christ's death for us judgment has already taken place.

Paul illustrates this in his letter to the Galatians. He states that on the cross Jesus became "a curse for us—for it is written, 'Cursed be every one who hangs on a tree.'"[1] In the Old Testament, after a man had been put to death for a capital crime, his body was hung in public to indicate that he had been cursed by God.[2] The people associated the curse of death and the person accursed so closely that they believed that the criminal himself had become a curse.

This is why Paul says that Christ has become "a curse for us." The fact that Jesus was publicly executed on a cross meant that he had been cursed by God. He took the judgment which we should have received for our sin. And because he did, we are freed from experiencing that judgment.

We will all appear before the judgment seat of Jesus Christ at the close of history, but this judgment has to do with our rewards, not with our ultimate destiny. Our destiny is assured. God has declared us clear of guilt. But how do we know it? How can we be sure?

The Resurrection—God's Assurance of Grace

The bodily resurrection of Christ following his death, the apostle Paul says, is the guarantee of our justification. Romans 4:25 says that Jesus Christ was delivered over to death because of our sins and was raised again because of our justification. God has accepted Christ's punishment, and he proves this by the Resurrection. The Resurrection is God's seal of approval upon the finished work of Jesus Christ. It's God's "Amen" to Christ's cry on the cross, "It is finished."

Think of what God's approval of Christ's death means. The penalty required by God's justice has been paid. We are cleared in court. The sentence of death which was to have been carried out at the final judgment has been commuted. We no longer tremble before God's justice as those "condemned already."[3] The final verdict has been announced: "There is therefore now no condemnation for those who are in Christ Jesus."[4]

What should our response be to what God has

32

done in justifying us through Jesus Christ? We should commit our lives to him in faith. There's no need for living in guilt. There's no need for all our attempts at self-justification. Don't boggle at the wonder of God's grace. Just accept the reality of it. Justification is a great turning point in history. It's not rigid ritual that saves man any longer; it's not slavish attention to law; it's not attempting to solve the baffling mysteries of religious rite or spell. It's affirming that God gave his Son in our place.

The cross of Jesus Christ was the turning point in history because it made possible justification, clearance in court, acquittal before God. And it can be a turning point in your history. God makes all things new when he takes away your guilt, and he wants to do that right now.

Prayer: Gracious God, our Father, give me the freedom of forgiveness, the sense of being clear with you because of what your Son has done for me. In his name I pray. Amen.

My little children, I am writing this to you so that you may not sin; but if any one does sin, we have an advocate with the Father, Jesus Christ the righteous; and he is the . . . [propitiation]* for our sins, and not for ours only but also for the sins of the whole world.

I John 2:1,2

*The author prefers the Authorized Version rendering *propitiation* as a more accurate translation of the Greek word and the basic concepts which lie behind it.

CHAPTER 5

Wrath Turned Aside: Propitiation

Tell me something of your view of sin, and I'll tell you a good bit about your attitude toward life. If the word "sin" turned up in a word association test—the kind of test in which you are supposed to say the first thing that comes to your mind when a word is mentioned—what would you say?

I once tried this approach on a hippie in the Haight-Ashbury district of San Francisco. First, I used the word "justice." His answer was, "Negative, man. It's the fuzz coming to check on the acid." His attitude toward justice was based on one thing: his fear that the police would raid his place looking for psychedelic drugs. Next, I suggested the word "responsibility." His ready response was *guilt*. "You only feel responsible because society has made you feel guilty."

The word "sin" did not enter our conversation, but if it had, his answer would have been about the same. Sin, for him and for many, is the way society, and especially our parents have made us feel about things that are not really wrong.

For others, sin is relative, tightly linked to time and culture. What is branded "wrong" in one society may be perfectly acceptable in another. Standards change, these people hold, so there are no timeless abiding norms.

Then there are those who view sin only as sickness. Crime, lust, lawlessness, greed—these are expressions of emotional maladjustment caused by poor relationships with parents or brothers and sisters in childhood.

Now it's important that we recognize that there may be some elements of truth in each of these viewpoints because fairness with regard to other people's convictions is a basic Christian virtue. At the same time, however, each of these approaches has serious shortcomings.

The trouble with these and many other contemporary attitudes is that they blame our problems on someone else. "Society is at fault." "My parents didn't show me enough love." "Religious leaders are old-fashioned, moralistic, not in tune with the times." There may be tinges of truth in any of these protests. Society is messed up today and always has been. Parents are by no means perfect, and sometimes they inflict their own hang-ups on their youngsters. Religious leaders may react negatively to the changing times. But we should not buy the idea that all of our problems would be solved if we could just improve our environment.

Two great gaps stand out in modern approaches to sin. First, they are blind to the permeating, persistent, permanent character of sin. I once heard about a man who had a bit of Limburger cheese on his nose and went around complaining that the world smelled rotten. The problem was with himself, but he didn't know it. So it is with sin. It not only holds us in its clutches, it puts its fingers over our eyes so we are blind to our guilt.

The second gap in much of the modern understanding of sin is that God is left out of the picture completely. We define sin sociologically, psychologically, anthropologically—but not theologically. The tragedy of this shocking oversight is that it keeps man from facing either himself or God with adequate seriousness. That's a terrible mistake, but one we will avoid if we come to grips with the present topic, a central biblical theme: *propitiation.*

God's Wrath Against All Evil

To understand what the Bible means by propitiation, we have to examine God's attitude toward sin. The most forceful term used to picture this attitude is "wrath." We find this in Exodus: "You shall not afflict any widow or orphan. If you do afflict them, and they cry out to me, I will surely hear their cry; and my wrath will burn, and I will kill you with the sword, and your wives shall become widows and your children fatherless."[1] Frightful language, isn't it? Its very fury sends a shudder through our systems. But God is speaking, and we have no choice but to listen.

So seriously does God take his commandments, so deeply is he committed to the rightness of his demands, that he goes to drastic lengths to enforce them. The apostle Paul sums up God's disposition against those who play fast and loose with his law in these chilling words: "For the wrath of God is revealed from heaven against all ungodliness and wickedness of men who by their wickedness suppress the truth."[2]

The thought of God's wrath is hard for us to stomach, but it is a dominant strain in both the Old and New Testaments. We find it troublesome for several reasons.

Why
1.

First, we are prone to take sin so lightly that we are puzzled by God's anger. Excuses come easy to us. The dimness of our spiritual perspective screens out the awfulness of our sins.

But God knows better than we the toll sin takes on human well-being. Human dignity, human rights, concern for the weak and unprotected are of prime importance to him because he made man. No wonder his ire lashes out against the damage that sin does to human dignity and human decency!

Did you notice that the offenses which were so sharply denounced in the passage in Exodus had to do with afflicting the defenseless—the widows and orphans? Nothing grieves the heart of God more than to see persons he made and loves mistreated. His love for them shows itself in anger against the wrongdoers. For anything less than wrath to be God's response would be to sell short his most noble creature, the crown of his creation—man.

2. The second reason why we find it hard to swallow the Bible's picture of the wrath of God is that

40

our own anger is so temperamental, so spleenish. When we say "temperamental," we usually mean 90% temper and 10% mental. Our anger is hostile, vengeful, immature, bitter. God's is not. It is the way that his righteous, holy nature reacts to sin. We are apt to enjoy our anger—at the moment, anyway. It is our way of asserting our ego, of getting even, of taking satisfaction in hurting someone else. Paul senses this when he warns the Ephesians: "Be angry but do not sin; do not let the sun go down on your anger, and give no opportunity to the devil."[3]

Our anger opens opportunity for the devil to trip us up, and most of it is sinful. This is not so with God. His anger is the expression of his concern for his purposes and our welfare. It smacks not at all of temper or tantrum.

God's Dealing with His Own Wrath

If the idea of propitiation in our text reminds us of God's wrath against sin, it also encourages us that God himself has dealt with his own wrath.

Propitiation means the turning aside of divine anger in response to a sacrifice. When John calls Jesus "the . . . [propitiation] for our sins,"[4] he means that Jesus' cross has averted the judgment that should have come our way. The death of God's Son has made it possible for God to withhold his wrath from us as sinners and to call us into his family as sons. Similarly, Paul points to the intervention of Jesus "whom God put forward as a . . . [propitiation] by his blood, to be received by faith."[5]

41

God took his own wrath so seriously that he went to drastic lengths to enable himself to maintain his own righteousness and yet to accept us, in all our wretchedness, as righteous.

Disaster would have been our lot if God had not intervened. Our feeble attempts to placate God end up being insults. Like the struggling of a man trapped in quicksand, our futile flailings at appeasement only make the situation worse.

In the Old Testament God provided a meeting place between him and Israel. Annually the high priest entered the inner shrine of the temple, the holy of holies, and sprinkled blood on the lid of the ark where the tablets of the law were kept. This lid was called "the mercy seat." The New Testament word "propitiation" is directly related to this Old Testament picture of the mercy seat, the place where God met man and covered his sins. What a beautiful description this is of what Jesus has done for us. In him, and especially in his death, God meets man and offers forgiveness in place of wrath.

God's initiative does not end with his sending of Christ as the offering for our sins. God also grants to the resurrected Christ the position of advocate to continue to intervene for us and to plead our cause before God. John writes in his first epistle that if any of us sins, "we have an advocate with the Father, Jesus Christ the righteous; and he is the . . . [propitiation] for our sins."[6]

God's Grace Apparent in Propitiation

At the heart of propitiation is the grace of God.

Where sin is not held in horror, grace will be viewed with complacency. But when we realize how sin hurts God and harms us, we will treasure that priceless grace that brings our healing.

This means that propitiation is more than just an abstract doctrine to be discussed in an academic classroom. All theology, all doctrine, all teaching from God's Word is practical if rightly understood.

Moreover, propitiation is a truth to be celebrated. It means that God's love made it possible for him not to be angry with us. When his wrath should have consumed us because we fully deserved it, God himself intervened and turned aside his anger by sending Christ. Yet he did all this without compromising his own integrity.

Think for a moment about what our response is to all that God has done. His act of love in setting aside the wrath which should have issued in judgment calls forth our *love* in return. Not that our love can match God's, but what else can we give to one who has everything? Our love may be feeble and faltering, but it is the best we have.

Our response is *worship* as well as love. God's love has in no way degraded him, sullied his holiness or blighted his righteousness. He loves us beyond measure and yet is still the lofty, incomparable, majestic sovereign of the world.

Grasping what God has done through the propitiatory love of Jesus carries with it three conclusions. First, we are encouraged not to take sin lightly. Both the fervor of God's wrath and the cost of dealing with that wrath are magnets to draw us away from a life of sin. If we presume upon God's grace by sinning casually, we have failed to feel the impact of that grace.

Second, we can be confident of the effectiveness of Christ's sacrifice. "Not for ours only but also for the sins of the whole world"[7] is the scope that John gives to the cross. The whole world may not be saved. Tragically, many—even you—may refuse the offer that Jesus makes. But do not blame God for your refusal. The power of Christ's death is not limited. His grace is not in short supply. It is available to all who ask—even you.

Third, we are urged by the awareness of God's grace to share it with others. "The sins of the whole world" were on Christ's heart as he died, and he calls us to share his burden. We want to be part of God's mission in the world. Not a club, a clique, an ingroup, we are called by the cosmic Christ to make his name known wherever we go. We know the secret of the universe. A God whose wrath we deserved has reached out to us in love and not to us only but to all who turn to him.

Prayer: Thank you, Father, for being what you are: righteous, holy, loving. And thank you especially for taking me as I am: rebellious, selfish, crooked. Teach me today large lessons of grace as I think of the difference between you and me and of what you have done to resolve that difference. In Jesus' name. Amen.

Blessed be the God and Father of our Lord Jesus Christ, who has blessed us in Christ with every spiritual blessing in the heavenly places, even as he chose us in him before the foundation of the world, that we should be holy and blameless before him. He destined us in love to be his sons through Jesus Christ, according to the purpose of his will, to the praise of his glorious grace which he freely bestowed on us in the Beloved. In him we have redemption through his blood, the forgiveness of our trespasses, according to the riches of his grace which he lavished upon us. For he made known to us in all wisdom and insight the mystery of his will, according to his purpose which he set forth in Christ as a plan for the fullness of time, to unite all things in him, things in heaven and things on earth.
Ephesians 1:3–10

CHAPTER 6

Freed from Slavery: Redemption

A knowledge of the culture of ancient times often helps us to understand the Bible. The social and cultural situations were quite different in olden days, and one of the basic differences was the role slavery played in the life and economy of ancient peoples. Think of the stories you have read or the pictures you have seen of slavery—slaves roped together dragging great stones up earthen ramps to build the pyramids, slaves chained to galley oars as wheat was hauled from Egypt to Rome while cracking whips overhead try to speed up the stroke, women slaves in oriental courts exposed to crude indignities at the hands of drunken revelers.

And there were other slaves, too, who traveled to America in chains, lying crowded on decks eighteen inches high, who picked cotton, toted barges, and lifted bales. Tragic scenes these are, but the Bible uses them to remind us of our human predicament. Without God's help, all of us are slaves. The only question is, slaves to what?

Against this background, God describes what he has done for the human family. Because the only languages we can understand are earthly languages, and because the only societies and cultures we know are human, God expresses himself in terms we can understand. He bends over to speak to us; as the old hymn puts it, he "stoops to our weakness." Now if we make up our own figures of speech to talk about God, we may fall into the trap of idolatry, distorting God and shaping him after our ways and thoughts. But if we listen to his ways of expressing himself in the Scriptures, we will not go wrong.

One such Scriptural expression describing what God has done for us is *redemption*. Redemption tells us that we have been freed from slavery. The background of this term is the slave market and the ancient economic system mentioned above. Listen to what the apostle Paul says: "In him [Christ] we have redemption through his blood, the forgiveness of our trespasses, according to the riches of his grace which he lavished upon us."[1]

Sin Is Our Slave Master

The first point to consider is our slavery to sin. Note the emphasis on "bondage." "Everyone who commits sin," said Jesus on one occasion, "is a slave to sin."[2] You remember how King David lusted after Bathsheba and how his lust led to his adultery, and his adultery led to deceit, and his deceit led to murder. He started on one level of sin and dug himself down to a deeper one.[3] We know how sin traps and holds us, how one act leads to another in our lives. Gambling leads to theft, theft leads to lying, and lying leads to crime to cover up the original theft. The proverbial camel in the tent is mild and amiable in comparison to the way sin takes over our lives.

Notice that sometimes in the Bible redemption is from slavery to the law. In Galatians 4:5 we read that God sent his Son "to redeem those who were under the law." The law binds us to its harsh demands and yet it gives us no power to keep them. Law and sin are closely connected. Law invites sin. Where the law is given, sin abounds. We see a sign that says "wet paint" and our first desire is to touch it. We see a sign that says "Keep off the grass" and we're tempted to walk on it. A little girl said to her mother once, "Mother, when you say 'must' it makes me say 'won't' all over!"

So the point Scripture makes is that man is held both in the grip of sin and in the clutches of his own attempts to deal with sin. He's trapped either way. There is no exit that he can make for himself. The more he attempts to dig himself out, the more life caves in on him.

A Ransom Has Been Paid

Now there's no indication as to whom or where the price is paid. Many theories in the history of theology, especially in the writings of the early church fathers have suggested that the ransom was paid to the devil, but the Bible doesn't mention to whom it was paid. Instead, Scripture emphasizes the cost of the payment, not the one who receives that payment. It's Christ's blood that's paid. The shedding of blood is the giving up of life. In other words, where Christ's blood is mentioned in Scripture the emphasis is on Jesus' death—not as a token payment as animal sacrifices had been, but as the full payment.

The payment of our ransom, Christ's blood, shows both how much God wants to redeem us and how costly that redemption is. It also shows what a terrible master sin is and what kind of price it takes to extricate us from its clutches. What looks attractive, compelling, and pleasing turns out to be such a horrible quagmire that it costs the life of the Son of God to lift us out of it. Thus, when we talk about redemption and being freed from slavery, we're talking about freedom from slavery to sin at the payment of a ransom.

Freedom Comes from Forgiveness

There's an intimate connection between redemption and forgiveness. Coming to terms with God is what forgiveness is all about. It's knowing that we are loved by God himself just as we are. Sin doesn't go away of its own will, because at heart it's rebellion against God. It can only be settled by God's pardon. Sin is not stuff or substance that can be cremated or evaporated. It can't be dissolved in liquid and poured down a drain. It's a disposition of the heart and will for which we have to apologize when we've been wrong toward God.

Forgiveness means not only coming to terms with God, but being equipped for a fresh start. The load of guilt is gone, the chains have fallen off. A new kind of life is possible, one that has loving God as its aim and serving the need of our neighbor as its purpose. Sin has a way of snatching our attention, of keeping our thoughts fixed on ourselves and our pride or our predicament. Forgiveness sets us free to give priority to God and others. We are no longer concerned with covering up, with rationalizing, defending, or trying to escape our responsibility. We can face what we are and realize that God loves us in spite of it.

When we talk about forgiveness, we have to remember that sin has been dealt with but not totally conquered. We don't arrive when we are redeemed; we are on the way. It is direction more than destination that marks our change.

The effects of sin may yet remain. That's one of the tragedies of sin. The aches and pains that come from our dissipation, the effects of our alcoholism may linger long after the habit is broken. The person who has been crudely and lewdly immoral may have to live with the stale, dark taste of memories as the years go by. Yet he is clear with God. His sin has been forgiven, and he's free for a new start in life.

But redemption does not end there because the Bible goes beyond even forgiveness and rescue from slavery when it talks about redemption. In

Romans we read, "we ourselves, who have the first-fruits of the Spirit, groan inwardly as we wait for adoption as sons, the redemption of our bodies."[4]

This statement reminds us that there is a close relationship between sin and death. When man sinned in the beginning, death began to take its toll. Redemption is God's way of dealing with our entire human problem.

He handles sin, on the one hand, through forgiveness and death; on the other hand, through the complete redemption of the body. Either without the other would be incomplete. Redeeming the body without dealing with sin would be immoral, setting us free to have the energy and longevity to do what we want. But forgiving sin without redeeming the body would doom us to partial existence forever. But God does both. So great is his grace, so freely has he forgiven, so fully was the ransom price paid, so deeply committed was God to our wholeness and welfare that he fulfilled his entire purpose in redemption.

The God who would go to this length to save you will not double-cross you. He stands by his word. He has a huge stake in your redemption.

What has you trapped? What special problems do you have that need solving? God is able to help you. You haven't done anything God can't forgive.

Ultimately by the power of the Spirit and the Resurrection he will transform the weakness of your body into the likeness of the glory of Jesus Christ. There are no slips between God's cup and his lip. What he has begun he will carry on to completion at the day of Jesus Christ. Salvation is

God's business. Redemption is his ministry. He makes all things new, and he will make them new for you.

Prayer: Gracious God, our heavenly Father, open my eyes to the state of my enslavement and to the goodness of your grace that can set me free. Through Jesus Christ I pray. Amen.

But when the time had fully come, God sent forth his Son, born of woman, born under the law, to redeem those who were under the law, so that we might receive adoption as sons. And because you are sons, God has sent the Spirit of his Son into our hearts, crying, "Abba! Father!" So through God you are no longer a slave but a son, and if a son then an heir.
Galatians 4:4—7

CHAPTER 7

Received into the Family: Adoption

Have you ever thought that God is in the adoption business? One of the expressions used of God's relationship to those who trust Christ is *adoption*. In our day we think of adoption in terms of orphans or children of unwed mothers.

The biblical idea of adoption emerges from the same cultural setting as redemption—the slave market. Whether slaves were captured in war, purchased as goods, or given as payment on debts, they were treated impersonally. They had no standing in the household, no inheritance. They were like property, below the level of the family, perhaps slightly above the level of the cattle or the camels, unless adoption took place. Then a slave could become an heir.

Ancient Babylonian texts tell us about the adoption of slaves, and the Bible itself contains a very interesting illustration of this. Abraham had a slave called Eliezer of Damascus, and we read that Abraham said, "Behold, thou hast given me no offspring [that is, God had not sent him heirs]; and a slave born in my house will be my heir."[1] The normal adoption formula in the Middle East was undoubtedly used in the relationship between Abraham and Eliezer. The master would say to the slave, "You are my son; today have I begotten you." In other words, "Today and from now on you bear the same relationship to me as though you were my natural son." The slave would probably respond to the master who was adopting him, "Now you are my father."

In previous chapters we've seen some of the metaphors that express the relationship between God and man. God is involved in this relationship, but human language has to be used since we have no divine language. We don't really know how God would talk about these things within the fellowship of the holy Trinity. We only know the language which he himself gives us to help us understand the gospel. We saw, for instance, that when we talk about salvation we can talk about being cleared in court or being *justified*. We saw that Jesus' cross is the ground of our justification and the resurrection is its guarantee. We saw that God in his grace has freed us from slavery, and thus we are *redeemed*. Christ's death is the price of this redemption, and God's grace is its source. We no longer fear God's wrath for Christ's sacrificial death has freed us from it.

Another startling aspect of the gospel is that we are received into the family of God. We are adopted by God. Listen to the words in Galatians: "But when the time had fully come, God sent forth his Son, born of woman, born under the law, to redeem those who were under the law, so that we might receive adoption as sons. And because you are sons, God has sent the Spirit of his Son into our hearts, crying, 'Abba! Father!' So through God you are no longer a slave but a son, and if a son then an heir."[2] Notice the contrast between slavery and sonship, between servitude and adoption.

A Shared Sonship

Jesus Christ is God's eternal Son by nature. We become God's sons by grace. Our sonship speaks of intimacy. As Jesus once said, "No one knows the Father except the Son and anyone to whom the Son chooses to reveal him."[3] I was raised in a family with older brothers and sisters. I learned a great deal about the secrets and the ways of my parents from the older members of my family. In the same way, Christ as elder brother in God's family lets us in on the Father's secrets. He shares with us the intimacy of his relationship with his Father.

But it is not only intimacy that is involved, but authority. To be a son of God means to a certain extent to share God's authority. It means to have privileges beyond the privileges of a slave. When I was a boy, we owned two cars. It wasn't because we had a lot of money, but because we were poor and could afford only old cars. One of them was almost always in the garage for repairs, so we had to have two. My father would send me to the garage saying, "You pick up the car. I think it's ready." And I would say to the mechanic, "Is Mr. Hubbard's car ready?" He would say, "Who are you?" I would reply, "I am his son." I spoke in the authority of my father, and the garage superintendent would then hand me the keys—and the bill. Intimacy, authority, and obedience are involved in our sonship.

An Abiding Spirit

We enjoy not only a shared sonship, but also the presence of an abiding Spirit. God sent forth his Spirit into our hearts crying, "Abba! Father!" Scholars have shown that this term "Abba" had not been used for God until the time of Jesus Christ. In other words, it was not until the Son came that we could learn to call God by this intimate name, which in our day would be something like "Daddy."

Contrast this with the chariness of the Jews before the time of Christ who refused to call God by his name. God was too holy to be addressed directly by sinful men. They used all kinds of other expressions like Heaven and the Name. But Jesus said, "Call him Father."

The sending of the Spirit gives us the assurance that we are related to God in Jesus Christ. God sends the Spirit to welcome us into his family and to remain with us for forgiveness, guidance and power. Think how wonderfully personal this relationship is. God, the Spirit, is actually present with us and dwelling in us, telling us that we are newly adopted members of God's family. This is not second-class citizenship, but a genuine, firm, warm family tie.

A Sure Inheritance

Beyond our shared sonship and the abiding presence of the Spirit of God, there is a sure inheritance.

This is a key emphasis of adoption. The social and cultural background of adoption is slavery, and the purpose of adoption in the Bible world was different from our purpose today. When we adopt children, it's usually because we have compassion upon them in their loneliness or we want to satisfy our paternal and maternal urges. But in the ancient world the purpose of adoption was to guarantee the continuity of the family, to preserve the name of the father and to see that his property remained closely tied to his name.

Think of what inheritance meant to a slave. No longer could he be sold or cruelly mistreated. Now he was part of a family with all of the great privileges and weighty responsibilities that sonship entailed. His whole destiny was transformed and settled by adoption. And that is what the Bible says about us.

God gives us a divine inheritance. We are heirs to all the glories he has in store for his own family. We share Christ's inheritance. We are joint-heirs with Christ. In the ancient world the adopted slave and the natural son shared together if the father willed it that way. And this is what God has done for us in his grace.

Our inheritance is guaranteed by the Holy Spirit's presence within us. The Spirit is God's down payment reminding us and assuring us that the final inheritance is being preserved for us by God himself.

Redemption and adoption go hand in hand. Both of them speak of release from slavery. Redemption emphasizes the release which is bought at a high price while adoption spotlights the new relationship with its guarantee of an inheritance. Redemption has an eye on the past from which we have come, while adoption looks to the future. It reminds us of where we are, what we have in Jesus Christ, and where we are going.

We can't close without saying a word about the joy of belonging to God. The Scripture says, "For my father and my mother have forsaken me, but the Lord will take me up."[4] This is better than a lodge, a club, a neighborhood, a school, or a team. This is God's family. As heirs of God we share with his Son, we call God "Father," and we're tied to him by his Holy Spirit.

Can you remember what it meant to you to belong? The boyhood club? The neighborhood team? The school drama group? I remember writing to a radio broadcast when I was a little boy and getting a badge that told me I was a Junior Birdman of America. Sometimes I'd get a Jack Armstrong pin or a Little Orphan Annie ring. There was nobody prouder and sharper in the neighborhood than I was when I had a badge or ring of membership. I was accepted in the group, part of the gang.

Think of how much more it could mean to belong to God, to bear the mark of his love. How about it? Wouldn't you like to be adopted by God —right now? Let's talk to him about it.

Prayer: Heavenly Father, I thank you that you have received me into your family, that you have given me your name and that you have taken me as your son or daughter. Now I ask that you make all things new in my own life and the lives of those who listen to your words. Through Jesus Christ, your Son, I pray. Amen.

Therefore, if any one is in Christ, he is a new creation; the old has passed away, behold, the new has come. All this is from God, who through Christ reconciled us to himself and gave us the ministry of reconciliation; that is, God was in Christ reconciling the world to himself, not counting their trespasses against them, and entrusting to us the message of reconciliation. So we are ambassadors for Christ, God making his appeal through us. We beseech you on behalf of Christ, be reconciled to God. For our sake he made him to be sin who knew no sin, so that in him we might become the righteousness of God.
II Corinthians 5:17—21

CHAPTER 8
Relationship Restored:
Reconciliation

There's an Old Testament story that illustrates a common human problem. The problem is sharp competition, fierce rivalry between brothers, and the story features the two sons of Isaac—Jacob and Esau by name. The Bible tells us this story in four acts.

Act I is Jacob's treachery. You remember the two great episodes of trickery where Jacob pulled slick deals on his older brother, Esau. Genesis 25 recalls a time when Esau, an avid hunter, came home from the country famished. Jacob took full advantage of his brother's hunger to drive a hard bargain for Esau's birthright. The birthright of the older brother usually meant a double portion—twice as much as the others inherited. This the desperate

Esau foolishly sold for a pot of red beans. Later Jacob conspired with his mother, Rebekah, to defraud Esau out of his father's deathbed blessing. Esau was whipped again.

Esau, chagrined at the loss of his father's blessing, takes us into Act II of the story: his threat of vengeance. By mistake Jacob had been given the upper hand in the family and the lion's share of the goods. Esau wept first, and then weeping gave way to hatred as he vowed to kill his brother. Jacob feared for his life and fled to the East where he lived with his uncle, Laban, for twenty years. After this time of exile, Jacob took his family and flocks and headed west to his home in Canaan.

This leads to Act III: Jacob's overtures of peace. Offended, wounded people can have long memories, and Jacob assumed that Esau had been nurturing his grudges for two decades. So Jacob sent messengers to offer gifts to his brother to appease his anger. The messengers brought back the ominous word that Esau's men—400 strong—were on the march toward Jacob's caravan. You can imagine Jacob's panic as he saw his brother's troops press toward him.

Act IV—the reunion—is next. Doing his best to protect his family, Jacob went out to meet his brother Esau. As the two men approached each other, the drama heightened. Then Esau broke into a run and the two strong men embraced. Brothers who were enemies for twenty bitter years were now reconciled.

The new relationship between Jacob and Esau reminds us of the striking, startling changes which

God works in our lives when he saves us. We've been considering the bright facets of our salvation, the way in which God makes all things new. You recall that God uses illustrations from human experience to describe these bright facets of our salvation.

From the field of law, for instance, he uses the term *justification,* which means that we are cleared in court. From the culture of the ancient world in which slavery played such a key part, he draws two terms: redemption and adoption. Redemption speaks of the release from slavery to sin, and adoption spotlights the slave's reception as a member of God's family. Now we see another bright facet of our salvation—reconciliation, the Bible calls it, a term drawn from family life. As we saw in the story of Jacob and Esau, reconciliation means a relationship restored.

One of the great New Testament passages on reconciliation is: "Therefore, if any one is in Christ, he is a new creation; the old has passed away, behold, the new has come. All this is from God, who through Christ reconciled us to himself and gave us the ministry of reconciliation."[1]

God Is the Source of Reconciliation

"All this is from God"—that's the first point to make. Throughout the Bible God takes the initiative in bringing man to him. Note the contrast here with the story of Jacob and Esau. In that picture the one who had done the wounding took the initiative. The guilty party, Jacob, sought Esau's favor. But with God the picture is the other way around. He takes the lead in restoring friendship even though the quarrel between him and man is not his fault.

This always is the biblical pattern. Adam was hiding in the garden, and God sought him out. Abraham was not seeking God, but God chose him. Moses was not looking for a religious experience, but God stopped him in his tracks at the burning bush. David didn't volunteer to become king, but God recruited him. Amos, the prophet, was not trained for his work, but God laid a hand on him and pushed him into it. And when we come to the New Testament, we see the virgin birth of Jesus Christ, the great sign of divine initiative, the tremendous reminder that what man could not do for himself, God did. "All this is from God," the apostle Paul says. And it has to be from God.

It's part of reconciliation that God shows his grace despite our sin. From start to finish the theme of the Bible is God's grace. He does for us what we don't deserve. That's not to say God takes sin lightly, for God hates sin. Before he can welcome the rebel, before he can receive the prodigal, he has to deal with sin. In his love and grace he comes to us in Jesus Christ and bears the judgment for our sin.

Sin is crippling. Man can't come to God on his own. Sin fogs our judgment, slows our reflexes, clouds our discernment, dulls our senses. It distorts our perspective so we can't see how bad we are and how good God is. It paralyzes our abilities so we can't always do what's right even though we think we know what to do. If there's a way out, God has to find it for us, and he does.

The message of the Bible is not that man seeks God but that God seeks man and finds him. If we are to be a new creation, we ought to say with Paul, "All this is from God." He is the source of our reconciliation.

Christ Is the Agent of Reconciliation

In II Corinthians 5:18,19 we read that God through Christ reconciled us to himself and that God was in Christ reconciling the world to himself. The God-man became the mediator. In him God's love and God's holiness were so combined and so expressed that man could come to grips with God on understandable terms. Man knew what God was like because he had seen the God-man.

When we talk about Christ as mediator, we shouldn't think of him as arbiter, a third party, a neutral neighbor. Christ's mediation is not like the government arbiter who sits down at a table with industry on the one side and labor on the other and tries to bring two hostile parties together. God was in Christ actively pursuing the task of reconciling man to himself as a concerned party.

No biblical passage ever speaks of God's being reconciled to man. In most human quarrels the blame is spread on both sides. Rarely is there a completely innocent party. Reconciliation usually takes place by compromise. But this is not so with God. Sin has to be dealt with, or God will be untrue to himself. But he himself deals with it. God was in Christ, and the way is clear for man to come home.

The Homecoming Brings Changes

The transformation brought about by this reconciliation is expressed in verse 17: "If any one is in Christ, he is a new creation; the old has passed away, behold, the new has come." Old ways of looking at life, old values and priorities, old goals and purposes are transformed. Worship becomes our aim; love becomes our purpose in life. Our direction is turned around. We begin to see life from God's point of view.

And all this is possible because our sin is dealt with. "For our sake, he made him to be sin who knew no sin, so that in him we might become the righteousness of God."[2] We treat sin as unimportant, as though we could readily cope with it; or we fear sin as though there were no remedy, as though its grip on human life were unbreakable. We know that sin is terrible. The most righteous man who ever lived had to be tarred with the brush of our sin in order to set us free. But sin is defeated. Its back is broken. God himself has taken direct, personal action to handle it. He sent Christ as our substitute. He became what we are—burdened by sin—that we might become what he is—wholly acceptable to God. He ended our quarrel with God by dealing with the cause of our quarrel—our sin. The way back is open. This is what the Bible says. So why not come home?

What a marvelous picture of the bright new

ways of God. Get the picture clear. Tune out the fuzziness of your fantasies. God has made it plain: your salvation is rich and complete. Jesus does save. You are cleared in court. The judge has paid the penalty, and he wants you to accept your pardon. You are freed from slavery. The selfishness, the rebellion, the immorality, the bitterness that choke you with their chains are shaken loose. Your days of slavery are over. You are received into God's family, adopted as a son, privileged to call God Father, a full heir to all that God has for those who belong to him.

You are restored to full fellowship with him. The quarrel is settled, the barriers are leveled, the tensions are resolved. The stranger has joined the family. God on his own, because of his love, has dealt with your debt, settled your account, bought your freedom, opened his arms in love to receive you. What are you waiting for? All that's missing is your response. Ask and you'll receive. That's the message of the gospel. The Lord of the universe, your Father, says "Welcome home!"

Prayer: God our Father, today please hear the prayer of all those who are taking their very first steps toward home. Through Jesus Christ our Lord. Amen.

May the God of peace himself sanctify you wholly; and may your spirit and soul and body be kept sound and blameless at the coming of our Lord Jesus Christ. He who calls you is faithful, and he will do it.
I Thessalonians 5:23,24

CHAPTER 9

Set Apart for Love: Sanctification

"What's so different about Christians?" That's a good question and one that deserves more than a superficial answer.

In a host of ways Christians may look and act like the people among whom they live. They drive the same cars, shop in the same markets, send their children to the same schools, and read the same newspapers as their neighbors who have not yet trusted God for his forgiveness.

In most cultures there is no distinctively Christian dress, hairstyle or language. See a couple walking down the street together, and there is no sure way of telling whether or not they are believers. Watch a secretary type a letter or a carpenter hang a door, and there may be no clear clue of his or her spiritual commitment.

How then is a Christian different from those around him in the world? The key difference between a Christian and a non-Christian is not so much a difference in sin (though there should be that), but a difference in forgiveness. The Christian has sought and received forgiveness from God. He says, as the old gospel song puts it, "I'm only a sinner saved by grace."

How God saves sinners is what the Bible is all about. The new birth, justification, redemption, adoption, and reconciliation are some of the ways in which the Bible describes this saving work of God. A new relationship with God can be established because our sin has been dealt with. And all this is made possible because Jesus took on our humanity, died and rose again.

This salvation process has a facet to it that is easily overlooked. God has not only rescued us from our desperate predicament of rebellion and selfishness, but he seeks to refine us and use us for his purposes.

This process of refinement and growth, a vital part of God's saving task, is called "sanctification." This rather overpowering word means simply God's work of setting us apart from the world for his particular use and service. This setting apart makes us different from the world in ways that we will see shortly.

Correcting Some Misconceptions

From our background and training we all bring differing connotations to a term like this. To understand what is meant by sanctification, it is helpful to correct some common misunderstandings of it.

Sanctification is not at all legalistic. Legalism is the mistaken idea that we gain God's favor by keeping rules or regulations. It says, "Do this and you will be sanctified." But sanctification does not rest on *our* achievements.

In the Old Testament, sanctification and law-keeping were more tightly tied together than in the New Testament. To impress on his people the meaning of God's holiness, his otherness, his difference from them, God set up regulations for Israel to obey and enforced them stringently. In the temple, for instance, certain vessels could only be handled by the priests for religious purposes. They were set apart from everyday use. Only the priests could enter the holy place with its lampstand and table of shewbread, and only the high priest could approach the ark kept in the inmost shrine of the temple as the symbol of God's presence.

Violation of these rules as well as those of diet and dress incurred dire judgment. God was using these tangible means to instruct his people in his and their uniqueness. He was no ordinary God, and they were no ordinary people.

But all this has changed since Jesus came. Holiness is not a matter of custom or costume, of diet or ritual. Christ has pleased God for us, and we are acceptable to God through him and only through him. This is the heart of the gospel, which makes it abundantly clear that sanctification, our growth in holiness, is not legalism.

Sanctification is not primarily negative. Being set apart for God's use is more than a matter of "don'ts." Of course, there are negative aspects to the holiness to which God calls us. No man can be set apart for God and at the same time glibly engage in questionable conduct. Peter calls his readers to drop their old way of life—"the passions of your former ignorance"—and uses as his incentive God's mandate: "You shall be holy, for I am holy."[1] Similarly, Paul lays it on the line with the Thessalonians: "For this is the will of God, your sanctification." Then Paul gets pointedly specific: "That you abstain from immorality; that each one of you know how to take a wife for himself in holiness and honor, not in the passion of lust like heathen who do not know God."[2]

Christian liberty does not mean we are libertines. But surely more is involved in holiness than just not doing certain things.

Experiencing a Divine Process

Sanctification is not primarily negative. A Christian is set apart *from* certain things in order to be set apart *for* something else. A divine process is underway, and its operation is a beautiful thing to behold—and to experience.

The work of the God of peace is what Paul calls this process: "May the God of peace himself sanctify you wholly."[3] Here Paul is not so much commanding as praying. Sanctification is not basically our success or achievement, but God's gracious work within us. It is not mustering our energies, screwing up our courage, stretching our nerves. It is opening ourselves to the power of God who works in us "both to will and to work for his good pleasure."[4]

The title "God of peace" is a reminder that this growth is possible because God has brought us to terms with himself. Where we were mutinous rebels at war with God, he has brought about an armistice. And the one who made peace is working out the full implications of that peace in our lives.

The life of Christian love is probably the way to paraphrase what Paul means by sanctification. Listen to another of the prayers with which the pages of his epistles are perfumed: "And may the Lord make you increase and abound in love to one another and to all men . . . so that he may establish your hearts unblamable in holiness before our God and Father."[5] To "abound in love" and to "increase in holiness" go hand in hand.

The prophet Hosea caught this connection between love and holiness in a remarkable passage. God is grappling with himself as to whether he will judge Israel or not. He has every right to do so, indeed, for Israel is guilty of disobedience at a hundred different points. Finally, however, his love leads him to withhold judgment: "I will not execute my fierce anger . . . for I am God and not man, the Holy One in your midst, and I will not come to destroy."[6] The Holy One is the Loving One. That is the word of Hosea and Paul. God's Spirit within us is called Holy, and his first fruit is *love.*[7]

The thoroughness of God's work of sanctification is stressed by Paul in our text: "May the God of peace himself sanctify you wholly; and may your spirit and soul and body be kept sound and blameless."[8] We cannot chop our lives into compartments. There is no way to pigeonhole our spiritual responses. We are whole people. God has redeemed our persons, our entire beings. He wants every bit of our personalities—body, soul, spirit—to be set apart for love.

Right thinking, right attitudes, right conduct—all must be combined if true love is to be present. The Old Testament Book of Proverbs is an excellent illustration of the ways in which our faith touches every area of our living. Work, leisure, rest; relationships with men and women of all stations; stewardship of time and money; dealing with neighbors and enemies—all are tied into the life of love and godliness.

And they should be. God has a right to all that we are, and he wants to set apart all that we are for his loving purposes. The God who shows his holiness in love equips us to do the same. His thoroughness calls him to work in every area of our personalities. And it has to be that way. We either love with our whole selves or not very well at all. Fragmented love, partial love, love in word but not in deed, in idea but not in action, is not worthy of the name.

The guarantee of completeness is Paul's last word to us in this discussion of sanctification. The process may be slow. The graph of our growth may be up and down like the stock market in a shaky season. But God is at work and it's on *his* faithfulness that we depend.

Our march toward maturity will not be complete until Christ comes for us, but the God who has recruited us leads us forward day by day and will see us through to the end. Sanctification is not our work any more than justification or redemption are. It is part of God's great mission of salvation and will be accomplished by his grace and power.

The rate of growth may vary from Christian to Christian and from time to time. The end result will not be uniformity among believers—so that we all look and act alike—but conformity to God's Son. His love is the standard by which our maturity is measured. His love sets us free to be what God intended us to be.

God is trustworthy and he will complete his purpose. That is his promise. Our response is to be open and to seek his will and to be faithful in doing it.

What's so different about Christians? God has set us apart to love, and he will help us to do just that.

Prayer: I thank you that you are a God of grace, peace, and power. What you have begun in my life you are able to complete. Forgive my stuttering starts, my halting attempts to make myself holy. Help me to trust the power of your presence within me. I want to be open to the best which you have for me, and I know that that best is love for you and those around me. Through him who loved me and gave himself for me. Amen.

We know that in everything God works for good with those who love him, who are called according to his purpose. For those whom he foreknew he also predestined to be conformed to the image of his Son, in order that he might be the first-born among many brethren. And those whom he predestined he also called; and those whom he called he also justified; and those whom he justified he also glorified.

Romans 8:28—30

CHAPTER 10

Perfection Achieved: Glorification

When you read a book, it's considered a form of cheating to read the last chapter first, especially with mystery stories where much of the fun is the suspense of watching the plot unravel. Hints of the outcome are dropped along the way, and the pages are strewn with clues calculated to throw the reader off the track while at the same time luring him on.

But much of life is not like a mystery novel because, in our human condition, we have no last chapter available. We can discover a bit of what has gone on in the past by reading history. And we can gain some perspective on the present by watching current events as they are interpreted for us by the news media. But there's a dark curtain between us and the future. This is one reason that many of our young people, our so-called now generation, are totally preoccupied with the present.

What will the future hold? This is a chafing question, one that makes a lot of people "up-tight." Older people are concerned about their financial resources which are being devoured by inflation, about their deteriorating health, and about the gulf of language and culture which separates them from their young people.

Young people have their own worries. They are worried about choosing their life work in a world that changes so rapidly that a trade can become obsolete even while one is training for it. They are anxious about the future of world peace and the possibility that continued conflict will drag them into a military life for which they have no zeal.

And we can understand these anxieties. The future is baffling. That's why we can be grateful for the Scriptures that sketch for us the main outlines of the days ahead. Not that we know all the details, but we know how the whole story ends and we know our part of it. We have the last pages of the mystery novel in our hands.

One of the final chapters in God's program of salvation is called *glorification*. Basically, it means that Christ's glorification is shared with those who belong to him. It is the culmination of God's saving work which begins in the past with the new birth —that fresh start which we need so desperately—and continues day by day as God sets us apart for love by sanctifying us; that is, by causing his holiness to mature in us. A key Bible reference to this future state of glory is Romans 8:28-30: "We know that in everything God works for good with those who love him, who are called according to his purpose. For those whom he foreknew he also predestined to be conformed to the image of his Son, in order that he might be the first-born among many brethren. And those whom he predestined he also called; and those whom he called he also justified; and those whom he justified he also glorified."

A Glimpse into the Future

Like most scriptural themes, glorification has to be understood in the three tenses: past, present and future—or as we deal with them here: future, past, and present. God's plan of salvation rolls on toward the future and catches in its movement all who belong to God through Christ. God is leading us into his great future, and we need not be anxious about clutching to the past or despairing over the present.

The glory of this future which caps God's redeeming task is best expressed in terms of our relationship with Jesus Christ. The glory, the transforming change that the sovereign God will bring about, means that we will be with Christ and like Christ to the fullest extent.

With Christ. The separation which began when Christ ascended into heaven will be over. The imperfect communication which his people have had with him during these centuries of church history will be totally refined. "Now we see in a mirror dimly, but then face to face. Now I know in part;

then I shall understand fully, even as I have been fully understood."[1] All barriers are down, all frustrations past, all doubts settled. The loneliness, the unsettledness, the discouragement of living by faith have given way to the joys of living by sight. Full fellowship is now a reality. We are with Christ.

Like Christ. This is an even higher privilege. Think of being like Christ! We read of him in the Scriptures and stand in awe and admiration before his courage and love, his wisdom and power. We yearn to see those virtues perfected in us. Instead, we grovel in cowardice and spite, stupidity and ineptness, and long for a better way. The great hope of the gospel is not only that God will *forgive* us but that he will *change* us, change us to be like Christ.

The apostle John describes both our present relationship to God and the dramatic change yet to take place: "Beloved, we are God's children now; it does not yet appear what we shall be, but we know that when he appears we shall be like him, for we shall see him as he is."[2]

What a complete change this is—a change which affects every area of our person. The terrible toll that sin has taken is reversed, and all the perverseness and weakness of our fallen humanity are done away with. Even our bodies, which remind us constantly of our mortality, will be transformed. ". . . we await a Savior, the Lord Jesus Christ, who will change our lowly body to be like his glorious body."[3] The grinding processes of sin and death are halted. A life of power and glory takes their place.

90

A Look at the Past

This bright future, filled with the hope of sharing Christ's glory, is based on what Christ has done in the past. Our future glory is not a cloudy dream, a wisp of wishful fantasy. It is the inevitable outcome of the task Christ came to achieve. It is firmly fixed in the great events of Christ's earthly ministry.

The Incarnation. Christ's human life itself was a display of glory. Remember John's testimony: "And the Word became flesh and dwelt among us, full of grace and truth; we have beheld his glory, glory as of the only Son from the Father."⁴ In the midst of our broken, bewildered world men saw the glory of the world to come.

The Transfiguration. The glory of Christ was seen with startling clarity on the mountain of transfiguration. Jesus had retired to pray with his three closest disciples. All of a sudden his face blazed with radiance, and his garments became dazzling white. The transforming power of God chose this striking way of strengthening Christ before he went to his death and of giving his disciples a glimpse of his future glory.

The Resurrection. Then when the stone was rolled away, the graveclothes laid aside, and the dead body stirred to life, the glory of God shone again among men. When God raised Jesus from the dead, he was demonstrating ahead of time the power of his kingdom, the splendor of the coming age.

The glory that all of God's family will one day

know has already shown itself in Jesus' resurrection. The defeat of death which looms as so large a part of the future has already been anticipated. What God has done to Jesus' body, he will one day do for all who trust his love.

The Crucifixion. As hard as it may seem to believe, the Crucifixion is in some ways a greater proof of Christ's glory than even the Resurrection. In John 12:23 Jesus announces that "the hour has come for the Son of man to be glorified." It is the cross that he has in mind as the word *hour* indicates.

The cross was flooded with glory for Jesus because it demonstrated his perfect obedience. It was the pinnacle of the mission for which the Father sent him. What greater glory than to placard God's love before the whole world! What finer splendor than to do the Father's will to the very end!

By his obedience, Christ paved the way for the time when all God's people will share his glory and do his will. Our glorification is only made possible by what Jesus has done for us. The inherent, the ultimate glory is his. Yet, in his grace he has chosen to share it with us.

A Perspective for the Present

The future glorification of God's people is guaranteed because of what Christ has done in the past. But the future and the past are not the whole story. The process of glorification, of sharing in Christ's glory, which is made possible by Christ's saving acts in the past and which will come to full-blown maturity in God's great future, is going on right now.

Christ in Us. "Christ in you, the hope of glory" is Paul's description.[5] The connection between past and future is not left to accident. Between the times, between his coming in the past as Savior and his future coming as King, Christ is present with those who trust and love him—with his church, his body.

And his presence not only brings comfort but also produces change, growth, maturity. The process of sanctification in which God sets us apart for love is part of the process of glorification in which God ultimately shapes in us the character of Christ. Christ's presence with us in the present and our fellowship with him bring the change: "And we all, . . . beholding the glory of the Lord, are being changed into his likeness from one degree of glory to another; for this comes from the Lord who is the Spirit."[6]

Christ for Us. Christ is not only *in* us, he is *for* us. This certain note is sounded in our Scripture lesson: "We know that in everything God works for good with those who love him, who are called according to his purpose."[7] So intent is God on our glorification, our conformity to his will and character, our total transformation into Christ's likeness, that he has hedged us about with his love. No circumstances can come our way to sidetrack God's program.

His purpose in creation was to form a people who would display his glory, to let the universe know just what kind of God he is. His way of doing this was to make man in his likeness, to make him capable of thought, feeling, and choice, to make him open to rich and lasting personal relationships, especially marriage.

But man's rebellion ruined all this. So God's plan for salvation went into effect in all its phases from foreknowledge to glorification. And the outcome of that plan is assured. Paul speaks of glorification in the past tense as if it were already completed: "Those whom he justified, he also glorified."[8]

Christ is *in* us and *for* us. God's work of glorifying himself by changing us goes on at *his* pace, according to *his* schedule, and by *his* power.

In a church my father pastored, there was a rose-shaped stained-glass window. The church was very old and the window had been painted over time after time. Then the day came when the building was to be painted again, and my father decided that the window should be cleaned but not painted. Day after day the workmen scrubbed, brushed, and scraped. Layer by layer the paint that had accumulated over the decades was removed. We could see the original beauty of the stained-glass window begin to come alive. Finally, the last coats of paint were peeled away, and the sun flashed through the glass. The bright colors shone as vividly as on the day the window was installed.

Glorification is just this kind of process. Day after day God's Spirit is at work in us cleaning away the accumulation of bad habits, unworthy attitudes, inferior motives. From one state of glory to the next he takes us until at last we stand in Christ's presence and are completely, totally, perfectly changed to be like him. What we were meant to be we will be. This is God's work. He alone can do it, and he is doing it.

Prayer: Father, I thank you for the accuracy of the old hymn and for the assurance it sparks within me:

"Then we shall be where we would be,
Then we shall be what we should be,
Things that are not now, nor could be,
Soon shall be our own."

At your pace and on your terms, lead me toward that day when faith becomes sight, and the sight is my Savior's face. In his name. Amen.

After this I looked, and behold, a great multitude which no man could number, from every nation, from all tribes and peoples and tongues, standing before the throne and before the Lamb, clothed in white robes, with palm branches in their hands, and crying out with a loud voice, "Salvation belongs to our God who sits upon the throne, and to the Lamb!" And all the angels stood round the throne and round the elders and the four living creatures, and they fell on their faces before the throne and worshiped God, saying, "Amen! Blessing and glory and wisdom and thanksgiving and honor and power and might be to our God for ever and ever! Amen."
Revelation 7:9—12

CHAPTER 11

Rescue Completed:
Salvation

The Bible is a textbook on salvation. This is its chief subject from beginning to end. It centers on what God has done for man. It is the account of a massive rescue operation, a mammoth program of deliverance in which God is snatching those who trust him out of their skepticism, selfishness and despair, and setting them free to be his people filled with faith, love, and hope.

The apostle Paul underscores this central theme of the Bible when he gives advice to Timothy, his son in the Christian faith: "But as for you, continue in what you have learned and have firmly believed, knowing from whom you learned it and how from childhood you have been acquainted with the sacred writings which are able to instruct you for salvation through faith in Christ Jesus."[1]

Instruction for salvation—that is the purpose of the Scripture. It is not a textbook on science, politics or poetry. Though it may comment on a wide variety of topics, its crowning purpose is to tell men how to be saved.

The Old Testament deals with this topic of salvation, of rescue, of deliverance in concrete and specific terms. When the psalmists, for instance, beg for God to save them, they are usually caught in some particular predicament. Illness, opposition of enemies, physical danger, false accusations of crime, rash acts of sin—these are some of the plights from which God's people beg to be rescued.

Salvation in general terms is not stressed in the Old Testament because God has already delivered his people from Egypt during the Exodus and had established the terms of relationship with him in the law and the tabernacle worship. But the pointedly specific references to salvation teach us a good deal about the nature of God. He is concerned with all our problems—physical, emotional, intellectual, social, spiritual. We can bring them all to him. And he has the power to deal with them. No pit is too deep, no barrier too high, no enemy too vicious for God's mighty arm to intervene in rescue.

Put all the specifics of salvation together in the Old Testament, and you find that it is a highly comprehensive concept. It embraces all of man's needs. God who made man wants him to be whole, complete, mature. And his program of salvation is bringing this about right now.

The New Testament spotlights the magnificent scope of God's salvation by expressing it in three tenses: past, present, and future. In Romans 8:24

Paul uses the past tense: "For in this hope we were saved." In the great pivotal events of history—the Crucifixion and Resurrection—we were saved. The job is complete. We can add nothing to it.

And several of the great words of salvation that we have studied in this series also focus on the past —justification, acquittal in court; reconciliation, our restored relationship with God; redemption, our rescue from the slavery of sin. If we have firmly put our trust in Jesus Christ and committed our life and destiny to him, we can say with assurance, "We have been saved."

But salvation also has a present tense. It is not only a past fact in history; it is a present process in our experience: "For the word of the cross is folly to those who are perishing, but to us who are being saved it is the power of God."² When Paul says *to us who are being saved*" he is not doubting the effectiveness of what Christ has done in the past. He knows that the work of salvation has been completed by Christ. We add nothing to it. And he knows that the future is assured. God will consummate his work at the end of history.

But what he is stressing in the words "are being saved" is that God is at work rescuing, refining, restoring his people right now. There is nothing static about the Christian life. It is not just a matter of resting on the past or waiting for the future. God's salvation is active, dynamic. God is doing his good work in us day by day, hour by hour, moment by moment as we have noted in our study of eternal life, sanctification, and glorification.

But it is to the future that we look primarily in

this chapter; the bright, perfect, assured future described in the Book of Revelation: "After this I looked, and behold, a great multitude which no man could number, from every nation, from all tribes and peoples and tongues, standing before the throne and before the Lamb, clothed in white robes, with palm branches in their hands, and crying out with a loud voice, 'Salvation belongs to our God who sits upon the throne, and to the Lamb!' And all the angels stood round the throne and round the elders and the four living creatures, and they fell on their faces before the throne and worshiped God, saying, 'Amen! Blessing and glory and wisdom and thanksgiving and honor and power and might be to our God for ever and ever! Amen.' "[3]

Here with wide-eyed wonder we are privileged to glimpse in advance the completion of the whole rescue operation which has gone on through the long course of biblical history. This look at the future is one of the great acts of the grace of God. Hesitation, discouragement, doubt can be held in check because the final outcome of all that God is doing is already well known.

The Scope of the Rescue

The first thing that hits us as we gaze at this heavenly scene is the range of people present. God's rescue is tremendous in its scope. Just try to imagine the size of the crowd—"a great multitude which no man could number."[4]

From the beginning, God has been forming a

people, gathering a community, shaping a nation to praise and serve him. Now his work is pictured as completed. Every last one whom he has chosen through the centuries is there.

Some Christians worship in small churches with struggling handfuls of fellow believers. It is easy to get the idea that the church may die out, that the freeways of history have been relocated and now bypass Christ's church.

But look at this scene. There they are, the redeemed of all ages, singing glory to God around his throne. History's program is brought to a smashing climax, a dramatic conclusion in which the saving God and his rescued church are in center stage.

It's not only the number but the diversity that makes this multitude magnificent. "From every nation, from all tribes and peoples and tongues" comes the triumphant throng. Think of it. A program that began when one man, Abraham, was sent West from Ur of the Chaldees, has now swelled to include representatives from every political, geographical, and social entity on earth. It is a universal rescue by the Lord of the universe. All barriers of language, race, culture and economic status are broken down. And people from everywhere are united in common allegiance to God and to each other. Just to think about it makes us eager for our Lord to come.

The Heroes of the Rescue

The spotlight does not linger long on the multitude, thrilling as that company is. It passes quickly to the throne in the midst of the multitude and fixes itself on the God who sits on the throne, and on the Lamb. They are the heroes of the rescue.

Do not miss this. The rescued throng is not caught up in celebrating its own salvation but in praising the God who has saved it. There they are, "standing before the throne and before the Lamb, clothed in white robes, with palm branches in their hands" like the crowds on the first Palm Sunday. And their theme is "Salvation belongs to our God who sits upon the throne, and to the Lamb!"[5]

Not the fact of salvation, but the God who is the Savior is the focus of attention. Long ago a hymn writer said it well:

"The bride eyes not her garment, but her dear
    bridegroom's face;
I will not gaze at glory, but on my King of grace:
Not at the crown he giveth, But on his pierced
    hand;
The Lamb is all the glory of Emmanuel's land."
                    (Anne R. Cousin)

God is the hero of the Bible from beginning to end. He stood at the dawn of creation and spoke the worlds into being. His election made Israel a nation, and his might sustained her through the centuries. His love sent Christ to die for us, and his power brought him alive from the dead. His grace sent the Spirit to form the church, and his guidance will preserve and nurture that church until the end. "Salvation belongs to our God!"

But it also belongs to the Lamb. This is an important reminder that without Christ's loving sacrifice there is no salvation. Ultimately, what we are saved from is sin, and only the sinless Son of God could take care of that. Over this magnificent throne falls the shadow of the cross. In the midst of this splendid scene the Savior is called the Lamb. No sacrifices, no salvation. Salvation belongs to the Lamb. "There was no other good enough to pay the price of sin."

The Purpose of the Rescue

No wonder the heavenly courts ring with praise. The work for which God created the universe in ·the beginning has come to its full fruition. All that he intended has been achieved. All the enemies that sought to thwart his aims have been put down.

Now all creation can sing his praise. And this was his real purpose all the while: to form a people who would make known his glory to men and angels everywhere. So in the last scene, the redeemed are present, but so are the angels and so are the elders who represent the great heroes of the faith, and so are the four living creatures symbolic of the whole creation including the animal world.

The angels serve as spokesmen for the whole creation and say what we all feel when we think of God's high deed, his crowning task of saving a people to praise his name: "Blessing and glory and wisdom and thanksgiving and honor and power and might be to our God for ever and ever."⁶ And we do not have to wait for heaven to join this chorus. We can start singing right now.

Prayer: Thank you, Father, for showing me the end of the story while I am still on the way. The lamp of your Word not only brightens the path at my feet but lights up the whole trail clear to the end. May the clear picture of the outcome of my salvation hearten me to live as a saved citizen of that heavenly kingdom all along the way. Through Jesus Christ my Lord. Amen.

Now after John was arrested, Jesus came into Galilee, preaching the gospel of God, and saying, "The time is fulfilled, and the kingdom of God is at hand; repent, and believe in the gospel."
Mark 1:14,15

CHAPTER 12
The Great Rescue

What's the Bible all about? That's the question with which we began, and that's the question we've sought to answer in this book. The Bible is about God and about his Great Rescue—the rescue of his rebellious creation from the clutches of sin. It's about God's Son, Jesus Christ, and what he has done for man.

What happens when God reaches down to us in Jesus Christ and begins to turn our lives around? First, we are given a fresh start in life—a "new birth" Jesus calls it. God comes into our life, forgives us of our rebellion, and makes all things new. We begin a new life of serving God.

This new life is called "eternal life"; we are linked to the very source of life—God himself. It's a new kind of life, a life in which we experience God's love and forgiveness every day. This new life is available to us because we have been cleared in court; "justification" is what the apostles called it. Our guilt is dealt with and Christ's own righteousness is credited to our account with God.

Our justification was costly, however, for it involved the payment of a penalty. Jesus Christ paid the penalty that we should have paid for our sin. He gave his own life as a sacrifice to enable God to withhold his righteous wrath from punishing us. This is "propitiation."

The death of Christ was not only payment of a penalty, but payment of a ransom. We were slaves to sin, unable to please God. But Christ has freed us from slavery to sin; "redemption" is the bright word here. But more than this, Christ has freed us to become sons—sons of God with all the rights and privileges of that sonship. This is "adoption" into God's own family.

The sacrificial death of Christ also accomplished "reconciliation." God's wrath was God's righteous response to our sin. But Christ's death satisfied God's just nature and allowed God to withhold his wrath. This paved the way for us to come home. The loving Father waits for us.

Membership in God's family is only the beginning. A process of "sanctification" is underway. God sets us apart from the norms and standards of the world to love and serve him and his people in a new way. God begins to reverse the effects of sin and purify us. At the same time, God is at work to make us like Christ—"glorification" we call this.

This work of God will continue until we step into the presence of Christ; we will then be completely like him.

Finally, because of God's work in our lives, we face the future with great anticipation. The Great Rescue, begun by God millennia ago, will be completed, and all of God's people will gratefully praise God's goodness in his very presence. "Salvation" is the term for this.

These bright facets of salvation illuminate our understanding of what the Bible is all about. Running through each of them are threads which make up the fabric of Christian faith. The first thread is that *sin has to be dealt with.* We're guilty before the law; a sentence of death has been pronounced upon us. Or to put it another way, we're already dead because cf our sin and have to go through a rebirth—a fresh start. We serve a ruthless slave master from whose grip we need to be redeemed. There are barriers to full fellowship with God, and we can't come into his family or be reconciled to him on our own.

The second thread is that *salvation changes our relationship to God.* When we're justified, we're cleared in court; we're no longer guilty, but acquitted; our death sentence is nullified. The very life of God, eternal life, becomes our experience. We're no longer manacled by sin, but freed to serve God. We're no longer orphans or slaves, but members of the divine family. We're not estranged and alienated, but warmly and firmly related to God. We're on good terms with him. That's reconciliation.

The third thread is that *these changes are God's*

doing and not ours. It is he who clears us in court; it is he who brings us out of slavery; it is he whose Spirit starts our lives afresh; it is God who receives us into his family and restores our relationship with him; it is he whose grace restores our brokenness and fashions us to be like Christ. He takes the initiative. As the Old Testament often puts it, "Salvation"—salvation in the full sense of the word—"is the Lord's."

The fourth thread—and in many ways the most important—is that to all these changes *Jesus Christ's ministry is essential.* He bears our guilt. His life is the price of our freedom. He shares his sonship with us when we are adopted. His love on the cross shows us that the Father will receive us into warm fellowship.

These four threads woven together—our sin, the change in relationship which salvation brings us, the initiation of that change by God himself, a change that is effective because of the ministry of Jesus Christ—are what the gospel is all about.

But the gospel is not merely to be talked about and analyzed. It's to be experienced and enjoyed. It's one thing to read a fascinating recipe. It's another thing to eat a scrumptious meal. It's one thing to read about the gospel. It's another thing to experience its power and blessing.

God's great plan of rescue is a meal to which all men are invited to come and eat. Have you tasted the goodness of God's work in your life? Have you accepted God's invitation to experience personally his "bright facets of salvation"? God stands ready to make your life new, to rescue you from the prison of meaningless living if you will accept his invitation to become his child.

Perhaps this prayer will express your desire to taste of God's goodness. Make it your own prayer.

Prayer: Dear Heavenly Father, I thank you for all that you have done for me through your Son, Jesus Christ. The price you paid to restore me to relationship with you was staggering, unbelievable. Yet I face up to my need and accept what you have done. Please give me a fresh start in knowing you. Make me your child, and make your home with me. In Jesus' saving name. Amen.

Scripture References

Chapter 1
[1]Galatians 3:14

Chapter 2
[1]Paraphrase of John 3:3
[2]John 3:6
[3]John 3:5
[4]John 3:13
[5]John 3:14, 15
[6]Numbers 21:4–9

Chapter 3
[1]John 10:10
[2]John 4:1–43
[3]Mark 10:29, 30
[4]John 5:21
[5]John 5:26
[6]John 5:22, 23
[7]Galatians 3:13
[8]John 5:24
[9]John 5:20
[10]Romans 8:38, 39
[11]John 5:21

Chapter 4
[1]Galatians 3:13
[2]Deuteronomy 21:23
[3]John 3:18
[4]Romans 8:1

Chapter 5
[1]Exodus 22:22–24
[2]Romans 1:18
[3]Ephesians 4:26, 27
[4]I John 2:2, KJV

[5]Romans 3:25
[6]I John 2:1, 2
[7]I John 2:2

Chapter 6

[1]Ephesians 1:7, 8
[2]John 8:34
[3]II Samuel 11
[4]Romans 8:23

Chapter 7

[1]Genesis 15:3
[2]Galatians 4:4–7
[3]Matthew 11:27
[4]Psalm 27:10

Chapter 8

[1]II Corinthians 5:17, 18
[2]II Corinthians 5:21

Chapter 9

[1]I Peter 1:14–16
[2]I Thessalonians 4:3–5
[3]I Thessalonians 5:23
[4]Philippians 2:13
[5]I Thessalonians 3:12, 13
[6]Hosea 11:9
[7]Galatians 5:22
[8]I Thessalonians 5:23

Chapter 10

[1]I Corinthians 13:12
[2]I John 3:2
[3]Philippians 3:20, 21
[4]John 1:14
[5]Colossians 1:27
[6]II Corinthians 3:18
[7]Romans 8:28
[8]Romans 8:30

Chapter 11

[1]II Timothy 3:14, 15
[2]I Corinthians 1:18
[3]Revelation 7:9–12
[4]Revelation 7:9
[5]Revelation 7:10
[6]Revelation 7:12